AMAZING RESCUE VEHICLES

AMBULANCES

BY LORI DITTMER

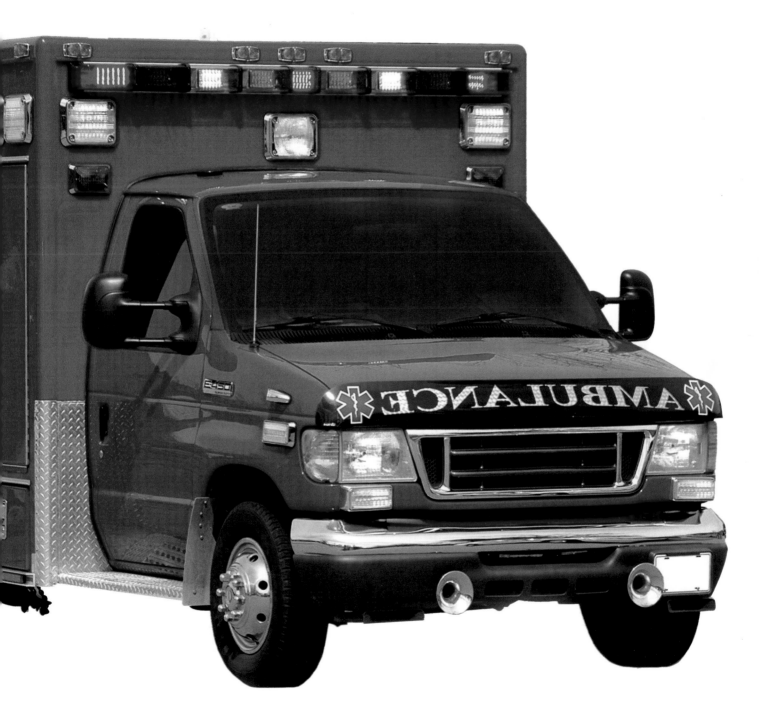

CREATIVE EDUCATION • CREATIVE PAPERBACKS

Published by Creative Education and Creative Paperbacks
P.O. Box 227, Mankato, Minnesota 56002
Creative Education and Creative Paperbacks are imprints of
The Creative Company
www.thecreativecompany.us

Design by The Design Lab
Production by Dana Cheit
Art direction by Rita Marshall
Printed in the United States of America

Photographs by Alamy (Old Paper Studios), Dreamstime
(Knightshade), iStockphoto (bluecinema, egdigital, FangXiaNuo,
FilippoBacci, OgnjenO, THEPALMER), Shutterstock (blurAZ, Stephen
Coburn, Digital Storm, Fotos593, jerrysa, Carlos E. Santa Maria)

Library of Congress Cataloging-in-Publication Data
Names: Dittmer, Lori, author.
Title: Ambulances / Lori Dittmer.
Series: Amazing rescue vehicles.
Includes bibliographical references and index.
Summary: A basic exploration of the parts, equipment, and
variations of ambulances, the fast-moving rescue vehicles. Also
included is a pictorial diagram of the important rescue vehicle and
its equipment.
Identifiers: ISBN 978-1-64026-041-2 (hardcover) / ISBN 978-1-
62832-629-1 (pbk) / ISBN 978-1-64000-157-2 (eBook)
This title has been submitted for CIP processing under LCCN
2018938942.

CCSS: RI.1.1, 2, 4, 5, 6, 7; RI.2.2, 5, 6, 7, 10; RI.3.1, 5, 7, 8;
RF.1.1, 3, 4; RF.2.3, 4

First Edition HC 9 8 7 6 5 4 3 2 1
First Edition PBK 9 8 7 6 5 4 3 2 1

Table of Contents

Ambulances are

rescue vehicles. They pick up people who are hurt or sick. They bring them to a hospital. Early ambulances were pulled by horses. They carried wounded soldiers from battlefields to doctors.

Horse-drawn ambulance rides were bumpy and uncomfortable.

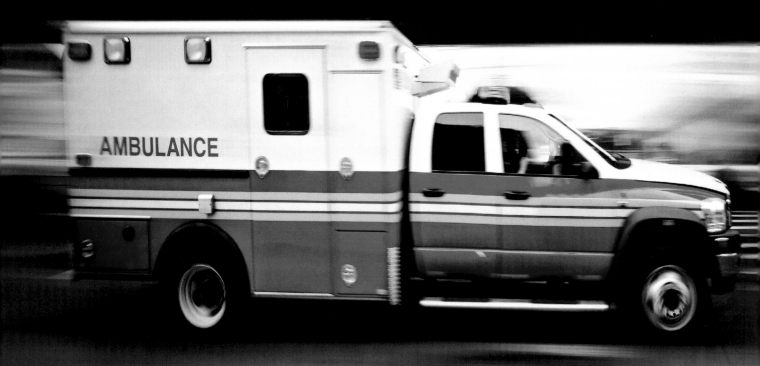

Ambulances can drive faster than the speed limit in an emergency.

Today, ambulances speed through streets. Lights on an ambulance flash in an **emergency**. **Sirens** blare. These tell other drivers to move out of the way. The ambulance needs a clear path on the road.

emergency an unexpected, dangerous situation that requires immediate action

sirens warning devices that make long, loud noises

Transport ambulances cannot carry as much equipment.

Some ambulances look like vans. They are often used for longer trips. They might bring **patients** from a small hospital to a larger one.

patients people who are getting medical care

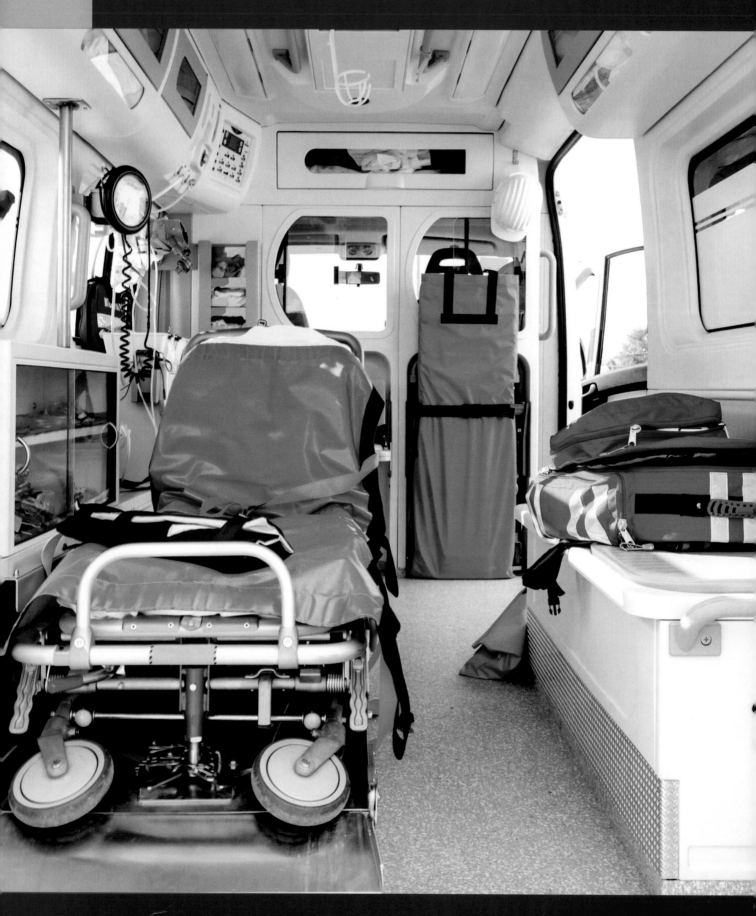

Supplies are kept in benches and cabinets in the back.

Other ambulances are more like small trucks. They can hold more equipment and people. A ramp sometimes helps the crew load the **stretcher**. Most stretchers have legs that can change heights.

stretcher a cart with a bed used for moving patients

Ambulances take patients to hospital emergency rooms.

In an emergency, people call a special phone number for help. For the United States, that number is 911. **Dispatchers** answer the call. They tell the ambulance where to go.

dispatchers people who receive messages and quickly send emergency services where they are needed

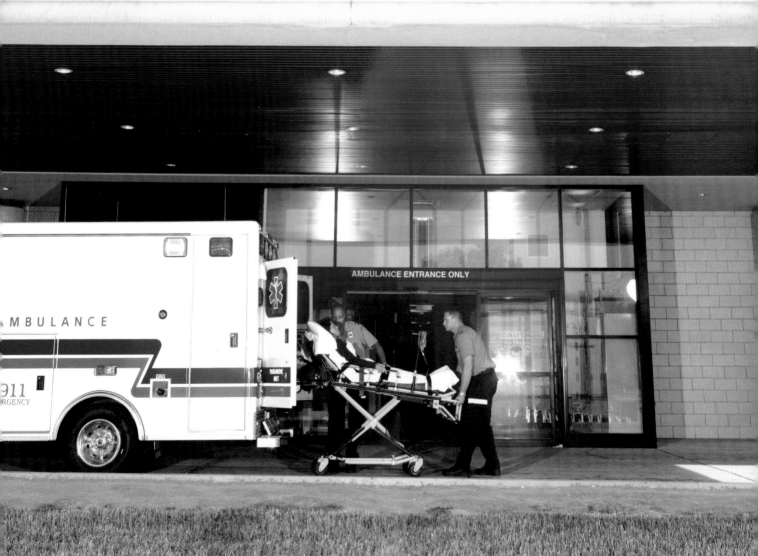

Most ambulances have a crew of two or three people.

One person drives the ambulance. The driver talks to the dispatcher on a two-way radio. Other **paramedics** and emergency medical technicians (EMTs) ride in the ambulance.

paramedics people who are trained to give emergency medical care

Paramedics and EMTs

are trained to help people in all types of situations. They care for patients on the way to the hospital. Neck braces and backboards hold patients still during the ride.

Doctors are ready to help the patient as soon as an ambulance arrives.

Ambulances are ready to go wherever they are needed. They rush to accidents and fires. They speed to homes and businesses. They stand by at sporting events in case someone gets hurt.

Ambulances use their lights and sirens only when there is an emergency.

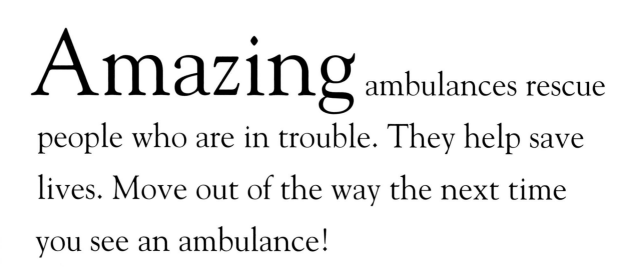

Amazing ambulances rescue people who are in trouble. They help save lives. Move out of the way the next time you see an ambulance!

Larger ambulances have room for a family member to ride along.

Ambulance Blueprint

star of life

tire

equipment door

AMBULANCES

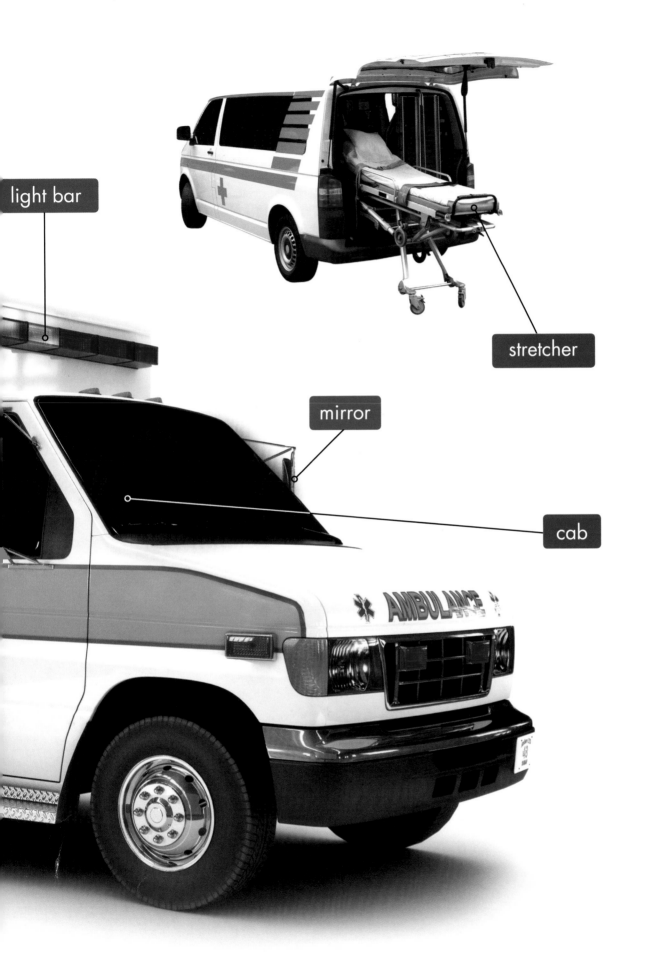

light bar

stretcher

mirror

cab

AMBULANCE

Read More

Dinmont, Kerry. *Ambulances on the Go*. Minneapolis: Lerner, 2017.

Murray, Julie. *Ambulances*. Minneapolis: ABDO Kids, 2016.

Websites

Kids Health: How to Use 911
http://kidshealth.org/en/kids/911.html#
Learn about emergencies and when to call 911.

Kids Want to Know About Ambulances
https://www.youtube.com/watch?v=RVXPqqZ0Xqs
Watch a video about what happens in an ambulance.

Note: Every effort has been made to ensure that the websites listed above are suitable for children, that they have educational value, and that they contain no inappropriate material. However, because of the nature of the Internet, it is impossible to guarantee that these sites will remain active indefinitely or that their contents will not be altered.